T0078080

Words

OF A

Widow

C. BAGER

BALBOA.PRESS
A DIVISION OF HAY HOUSE

Balboa Press books may be ordered through booksellers or by contacting:

Balboa Press
A Division of Hay House
1663 Liberty Drive
Bloomington, IN 47403
www.balboapress.com
844-682-1282

Print information available on the last page.

ISBN: 978-1-9822-6074-3 (sc)
ISBN: 978-1-9822-6075-0 (e)

Balboa Press rev. date: 12/21/2020

Contents

Monsters and Caffeine

Rest your head on me,
I will hold your pain.
I can numb it with my touch.
Nothing can hurt you now,
I'm a fortress for your heart.

Tuck your soul into mine.
Empty yourself,
unpack yourself,
submerge yourself into my love.

I am sturdy,
steady,
built to carry your anguish.
I'll carry it on my back because seeing you at ease makes
any burden light.
I'll tell you the most beautiful things about yourself that
you don't yet know.
I'll fill you up with such intensity that your soul will
break free from its chains.

I'll cover you,
I'll soften you,
I'm holding everything you are.
Where do you feel ugly?
Where do you feel abandoned?
Who pierced you and who made you feel less than?
It's never too much for me.
I'll shine love onto it.
Please don't skip a thing.
Is it easing up?
Do you know, there is nothing too dark in you that I
can't love?
I love your monsters.
Let your demons drink coffee with us.
Open the curtains.
I'm still here.

Whatever you've done,
no matter how lost you feel,
I'm permanently wrapped around you.
From now on,
if anything wants to hurt you,
it will have to pass through me.
And I am not afraid of your shadows.

Get Me Out

I'm strong.
I'm oppressed.
I'm deranged.
I'm manic.
I'm Zen as fuck.
I'm a master at mind games.
I'm oblivious to this world.

I know exactly who you are under that pristine exterior.
My mouth is stitched shut from trauma and neglect.
My eyes are blurred from all who spit in my face.
I'm still breathing, but it's a bit shaky.
I'm a clumsy animal trying to survive in this self-absorbed world.
Where are the creatures like me?
The ones who can make love to your soul before they
even say hello.

I'm roaming,
a defeated wanderer.
I'm taped together by the people who loved me enough
to make me smile.
I feel too much some days,
and other days I don't feel a fucking thing.
Not even you.
I'm a monster with a scared child hiding in its belly,
praying to God to get me out

Pour Me Everywhere

I watch you crack my heart open like an egg.
There is no resistance on my end.
I bite my lip as I slowly watch my hopes and dreams,
my pearls of tenderness,
the sparkle of joy in my life,
all pour straight into your filthy cup.
I watch you suck it down.
Struck with grief and jolts of pain,
I find a sense of relief.
It was my choice to let you consume me,
and I don't care how you break me,
as long as I can live within you.
Forever.

Ménage à Trois

Seeing you with her,
it is like no other experience.
I'm outside of myself as I watch.
I've literally left myself,
left my physical body because it already knows,
it is not capable of containing the ache that rises when I
see your hand on the small of her back.
But then again,
she is so fucking beautiful,
I could,
I would,
fall in love with her too.

High on Love

The night you kissed me in my car,
I thought I'd get pulled over for drunk driving.
You injected me with your passion for life,
and your drive to always do what was right and good.
And kissing me was most certainly the right thing
to do,
and very,
very good.
You ignited me to be a better person,
and now whenever I do what's right and good,
my lips tingle.

Let's Play 'House'

We were two scared and overly sensitive kids trying to
play 'house' when we moved in together.
We would show each other love through pain and
destruction which is all we knew.

But every now and then,
like a break in the clouds,
something so blindly beautiful would seep through.
It would swirl up through the debris,
soothing us and infusing us in a way only you and I
could possibly understand.

We were bonded in a love that began lifetimes ago.
How could I walk away from such a soul-level
investment?
Your imprints were far too deep to erase with time.
Our love was so dark,
but I would have stayed forever for that next
love-transfusion.

Safe Haven

I will wait for you,
like that loyal puppy at the door.
I will lay myself out like a red carpet,
welcoming you home to me,
and in me,
with the same goofy expression plastered on my face as
always.

Just like death and taxes,
you can be certain I'll always be around.
When you are tired and battle-scarred,
let me take off your shoes and warm you up,
just like a furnace.
I'll thaw out all your dread and sadness and you can
melt right into me,
knowing that wherever you go,
I will always be a safe home for you.

Broken Doll

I was seeing nothing but black.
You could have cut me open and I'd feel not a single sensation.
I was a lifeless broken doll.
If no one was going to put me out of my misery,
I sure would.

I wrapped the cord around my neck in a total haze,
knowing in death I could finally find you.
I was sobbing uncontrollably as this would be my last pity party.
In-between sobs,
something so gentle in the air brushed my cheek.
It wasn't a tear,
I checked.

I heard so clearly and distinctly,
"this is not your time."
And for once,
I felt the beating of my bleeding heart.
Even with no one visibly nearby,
I wasn't alone that night,
and I am eternally grateful.

Eyes Wide Open

You came to me in my dream,
popping up on me the way you would in real life.
Amused but shocked,
I gasped,
spitting out, "you're supposed to be dead!"
"Shh, you will ruin it," you said.
You told me to open my eyes and watch carefully.

I saw people dying,
but their spirits bounced back up out of their bodies.
This whole death thing wasn't what I thought it was.
Not even close.
I couldn't believe my eyes,
but knew that I finally understood what you were
trying to show me.
You smiled and turned away.
I woke up in tears.

Little White Room

"You should eat more," someone told me.
"All you do is sleep," said someone else.
"Why are you here?" asked the nursed.
"Nothing brings me joy and I don't have the will," was
all I could muster up through my bluish-
grey cracked lips.

My eyes had sunken in,
hair dry and brittle.
I hadn't brushed my teeth properly in days.
How could I have felt such despair so deeply that I
started to wear it?
I was ripping my hair out in chunks.
I was a walking corpse with no destination.

My mind is silently screaming all day long,
an internal noise I can't stand.
It's a two-way mirror,
I can't reach you and there is absolutely nothing you can
do to get through to me.

Imprisoned,
haunted,
shackled by painful memories.
The face of PTSD is not a pretty one,
it is merciless and unrelenting.

Amber Eyes

His eyes wide and innocent like a deer when we were
loving on each other.
So deep,
I was scared if I looked too long I would fall right in.
He shared his spirit with me,
a celestial world I became fanatical with.
He pierced me so sharply,
my handsome cupid,
I knew from that moment I would never truly be
anyone else's.

When hurting,
his eyes were bright amber,
with golden flecks.
He always had a silver tear that came out of his eye
every once in a while,
and I knew that meant he had experienced more pain
than a human being should be allowed to
endure in a single lifetime.

His eyes,
bright and captivating,
curved just like rainbows when he laughed.
His eyes told me all I needed to know,
but it took years for me to understand that they were his
only cry for help.

The Rescue

I was a sad and fragile bird with broken wings and a
mourning heart.
I had no sense of direction and no place to call home.
I measured time by my tears and my heart was locked
in a box buried under mounds of sorrow,
hatred,
desperation,
and confusion.

I had long forgotten how to love,
and affection had become a foreign concept to me.
Soft love was your expertise,
and soul-kissing was your language.
You were always a sucker for strays.
You upheld me,
nourished my spirit,
kept me alive,
and convinced me that I wasn't a mistake,
that I wasn't lacking anything.

My soul was hemorrhaging,
and you didn't give up,
not even once.
You fixed me up with a tourniquet of love,
and you enveloped me in your protection and promises
of infinite love.
You had arrived exactly on time.

Place of Refuge

I was a reckless,
feral,
promiscuous,
and volatile young adult with no self-control and I
couldn't stay in once play for very long.
Somehow you were amused by my ability to open and
share so easily,
no filter or boundaries.

You were the exact polar opposite of me,
but you never once judged me.
Instead I had grown on you.
All the times I had drank too much at a party,
gotten dumped by a rotten lover,
gotten stranded or just plain couldn't sleep because of
my neurotic tendencies,
you always let me in.

All hours of the night,
tapping at your window,
I would crawl into your bed and you just held me.
And you listened.
You were a vault for all my fears,
and your chest was a haven for my trickling tears.
Your bed was the closest thing to a sanctuary,
and you will always be my rock.

The Witch
Next Door

She is the scariest yet most deeply generous person I
have ever met.
She's a psychic witch that shows no mercy unless you
bare your soul to her.
She will easily extract all your darkest secrets and
terrorizing thoughts.

She will strip you of any falsities,
ripping off the mask you present to the world while
smiling.
On the other hand,
she will compliment and encourage you in a way that
you wonder why you ever doubted
yourself,
proving that you are stellar and profoundly important
to this universe.

She wrestles with demons and runs with angels.
She embraces whatever crosses her and takes it head-on
like a true warrior.
She uproots everything in her path just by existing.
Her outspoken, razorblade mouth will either dismember
you or fight like Hell for you.

Her purity and loyalty to the people she loves brings me
courage in this dark world.
Her indomitable will is contagious,
and she'll never know how much I admire what a
firecracker she is,
so dangerous but beautiful to watch.

Death Can't Keep Me from You

I speak for those who left too soon.
It goes something like this:

I know you loved me,
but I couldn't feel it,
or anything else for that matter.
I know you wanted me to stay,
but I didn't fit in there.

I held out as long as I could,
but the pain caught up with me and consumed
everything I was.
Don't you see I was dead long before I left you?
I loved you with every broken piece.
It was my choice that day.

I see you crying for me,
a mess scattered across the floor.
I'm sorry I hurt you by leaving,
but I was so convinced that your life would be better
without me and my depression resting on
your anxious shoulders.

Please know I'm closer to you now than I ever was on
Earth.
I can protect you in ways you won't even be aware of,
and I hear you when you call my name on the darkest
nights.

When you are sad and hear my song on the radio,
it's not a coincidence.
And when I sneak into your dreams,
it's only because I want to see you smile in your sleep.
I will make it up to you in other lifetimes.

We will have fun finding each other all over again.
For we will always meet.
I am your angel now,
and I will wait for you.

We've Been
Here Before

This is the life that you and I have created into being
over many lifetimes.
This is our tiny little universe weaved with our passions,
true devotion,
intricate expressions built into our own special
language,
tears and bloodshed.
So much blood shed for you.

We have fused our very souls into one another and now
we can't tell where it began or where it
will end.
We will keep transforming,
evolving,
but in this moment we are together.

All this time,
toiling,
yearning,
sacrifices we'd rather not discuss,
just to see your face in front of me.
Just to feel your heart beating in sync with mine.
It's a marvel to have you breathe into my hair and smell
you on my skin.
I want to breakdown and die into you,
all over again.

Handle with Care

Stranded to do this life on my own,
lost at sea without my captain.
This phantom heart lives in me now,
and everybody feels the gaping void within my chest.

Our life,
once vibrant and pulsating with magic,
washed away.
Our dreams,
now stripped of any future,
completely faded to black and white.
Everybody wants to help me,
but no one has crossed that bridge yet,
so how can they?
My grief is heavy,
all-consuming,
a thick smog that few can sit with.

The script of my life is your worst nightmare,
a reminder of things that can go wrong,
a darkness that people try to avoid at all costs.
No wonder it is hard to be around me,
I'm the fucking grim reaper.
I'm a broken heart walking down the street,
dragging the memories of love with me,
like a rotting carcass.
These memories are all I have left now.

All my days blend into one never-ending funeral of you,
and everything that reminds me of you.
I'm haunted by this mess you have left me with.
Nights are long,
full of soaked pillows,
gut-wrenching sobs,
praying for some sort of accident to remove me from
this sinking ship.
No one likes to be the one left behind.

Destination
Unknown

He showed up at my doorstep and asked me if I trusted
him to take care of me.
"I don't trust anyone," I muttered somberly.
He had grown tired of my apathetic ways.
He handed me my fuzzy pink sweater,
and my bag of favourite things then led me to his car.

I hadn't left the house in days,
the sun never shone so bright.
I felt like a fish out of water.
"Where are we going?" I asked,
feeling hurried and unprepared.
"Far away from here," he said with utmost certainty.
"I have so much to pack," I said in a panic.
"You need to leave it here,
it's too heavy for where we are headed,
it will only drag you down," he said softly.

His steady and strong hand reached for my shaky one,
the one that clung to anything it could grasp.
I took one last look at all I had accumulated in my tiny
lifetime,
and watched it get smaller and smaller in the review
mirror.
I exhaled and looked over at him with a cigarette
hanging from his mouth,
wondering if he had totally lost his mind.
Feeling my gaze,
he smiled and said, "buckle up sweetheart,
this is going to be one Hell of a ride."

A Love Letter
Unopened

I wish to be closer to you,
in anyway possible.
Writing is the only way I can do this now,
the only tangible evidence of a love once alive and
luminous.
So many times,
I want to give up.
I want to disappear.
My heartstrings are all knotted and torn apart,
and every morning my spirit breaks all over again.

But oh,
this love.
This love for you.
It just won't let me quit.
How can it be?
You are dead and something that is living still runs
wildly through me.
It is its own lifeforce and shows no sign of stopping.
If prayers work,
please hear mine.

Nothing can kill or diminish my love for you,
believe me I've tried.
This tells me our love was real,
more real than even you or me.
It was better than anything this Earth can offer,
too good to last.

My love for you inspires me everyday,
and it is still as deep and intense as the minute I laid
eyes on you.
I want to thank you for loving me,
not many people could.
May God keep you safe,
I treasure you now and all the days of my life.

Orb

Sometimes when I look up to the night sky,
I wonder if you can see me down here.
Maybe I'm dancing in moonlight,
maybe I'm watching our daughter sleeping,
maybe I've had too much to drink and fallen asleep on
the couch,
again.

Sometimes I wonder if you are watching,
laughing at some of the ridiculous things I do.
If so,
I'm more than happy to keep you entertained.

I really don't know where you are,
or what you can see,
but I pray more than anything,
that you see the little light in my heart.
It is always on,
always shining for you,
all the way down here.
Please see me.
I love you.

What Are You Waiting For?

You do know why these dreams won't leave you,
right?
They are an intrinsic part of who you are.
You tried to squash them,
you tried to erase them,
you tried burning them (that was a bad idea!),
You even slowly tried to suffocate them under your
pillow.

It must be exhausting trying to snuff out such precious,
delicate,
and crucial parts of yourself,
isn't it?
Who in the world do you think you are to deny,
reject,
and ridicule exactly what you were made to be?

Your dreams are pieces of you screaming to get out,
to have an honest chance at life.
What if I told you there was another way?
One without maiming or killing the twinkling little
planets inside of you.
Calm the storm within you,
be patient with your war-wounds.

Listen to your body,
every little yelp,
and sing yourself to sleep.
When your dreams wake up to discover that your body
is not a killing field,
they can be coaxed to flourish quite easily.
You can do this all without even leaving the safety of
your own bed.

Clean up what's inside of you.
Vacuum up the cobwebs.
Make your entity a nice spacious oasis for your dreams
to imagine,
and to wonder.
Soon they will gladly begin to work for you.
Your dreams are your inner children,
be sure to take good care of them.

My Treasure

You are like a resplendent glittering jewel I found out of nowhere,
and I want to keep you all to myself.
But beautiful things should be seen and enjoyed,

So,
I show you off to the whole wide world instead.
I don't mind stepping into the shadow of your light,
because just being proximate to you makes me feel like I'm worth more than rubies.
When you are crestfallen by the ways of the world,
fed up with people using and exploiting you for your beauty and charisma,
I will hold your place.

I'll be there to remind you of who you were,
before the parties and fancy clothes.
Because I know you.
I've memorized you for so long,
because I was there first,
at the beginning,
and that's the you that I love most.

Copycats

There are so many people out there to admire,
So many unoriginal thoughts passed around,
over and over again.

There's always someone else's song to sing,
someone else's light to snatch.
Why do we do this?
You cannot be anything like another person.
Your equipment is totally different,
you are constructed in a way that only you can
understand.

We spend so much time trying to mimic,
compare,
or study someone else's ways.
What a pity,
when you could bring something so unusual and
remarkable to the table.

Turn your eyes inward.
Eat your own food.
And finally,
inspire your damn self.

Now That I Know Who I Am

Now that I know who I am,
I am not afraid to peel back the layers of my soul.
I am mesmerized,
captivated,
enchanted with the kaleidoscope of my being.

I am not afraid.
I put on my shield of armour and I fight for the world I
love so intensely.
I realize I cannot lose.
I cannot die.
I cannot lie to myself any longer,
I have transcended into nothing but my wholesome
truth.

I am not ashamed of where I have been,
or whom I've touched.
The marks I left,
I left them for a reason.
I fought my way into this life,
and I will surely fight my way out.

The Purge

I felt your destructive ways approaching,
just like one feels an oncoming flu or accident.

Your lack of affection,
your inability to hear my sadness,
made me nauseous.
Your screaming hurt my ears,
and gave me a throbbing headache.
The stabbing of your words,
ripped me wide open from the inside out.
The bloody evidence of your abuse made me terribly
weak,
cold and sweaty.

You weren't finished hurting me until you made sure I
felt the aching pain,
in every single part of my body.
I kept trying to throw you up,
but you clamped my mouth shut,
just so I could swallow the trauma all over again.

You confined me to a cage,
decorated with terror,
laced with unspeakable fear,
and paralyzing anxiety.
I starved myself,
and I chewed my way out.

You are a foul,
sinister monster.
A poison I refuse to consume any longer.
I'll stick my fingers down my throat,
pull you out.
I will purge you at any cost.

Words Are
All I Have

Words.
They won't let me sleep,
they won't let me be.
They are hurling themselves so fast at me,
and I'm trying to catch as many as I can.
I like to keep the pretty ones to myself,
and save them for rainy days.

In my dreams,
my soul makes love to words.
They swirl around me like fireflies,
and bring me comfort when I have nothing to reach for.
My chosen words are strong,
precise,
genuine,
and powerful beyond measure.

Sometimes my words are like snowflakes,
they softly land on you and give you joy.
Other times,
my words are shrapnel,
deliberately hitting you where it will hurt most if you
cross me.

My words are like cotton candy,
sweet,
fluffy,
fun,
delicious,
especially if you taste them slowly.

My words are my history.
My words create my future.
My words mirror to you,
everything you feel but cannot speak out loud.
My words stand for the broken people,
the underdogs
and curse those to torment the weak.

My words protect me,
they will expose you if they need to.
My words are endless.
My words are medicine.
My words are sometimes clumsy but still encouraging.
My words are scribbled all over my heart,
multiplying like cells.
My words are all I have left,
the only thing you can never take from me.

Worship You

I removed my shoes and tiptoed up to you,
dropping to my knees,
I've finally found my one and only promised land.
I rested my forehead on your feet,
unbridled from any vexatious thoughts or feelings of
trepidation.
I've never had a sober mind before.

I have an insatiable thirst for everything you are,
and I have saved up this love all my life,
for someone like you.
It feels so easy to hand over.
You wish for the fragments of myself that I've withheld
from the world,
and I find myself adorning you with all of them,
leaving nothing hidden or obscured.

I lay out everything I am right in front of you.
You alchemize it all into tenderness and endearment,
even the hideous portions of my past.
Everything with you is virgin,
spotless,
and washed away of any earthly contamination.

I give thanks for every barricade you have broken
through,
every mind-twister you successfully mastered,
and all the poltergeists of my heart that you vanquished,
just me meet me here.

Because of you,
our love is noble,
blameless,
full-bodied,
unrestricted,
and just plain adorable.

We love with the innocence of children,
and your eyes are my windows to God.
I hold you in the highest regard,
and I am perpetually bounden to you.

Messy Sheets, Or Just A Mess?

I look at our unmade bed,
the one with the sheets still shaped like you.
Not once did it occur to me,
that it would be the last time I would hold you.

You stomped all over the village of our life,
you washed away our history,
and then you set fire to all our memories.

You managed to demolish a love that was years in the
making,
and a heart that invested and entrusted itself to you.
And all it took was one kiss.

I'm left to sweep up all the rubble and spoilage that you
dumped on me,
and I've never hated anyone more than I do you.

The Eternal Boomerang

Here I am,
crawling back to you,
like a sad,
pathetic,
clown.

I don't know what's worse.
The way you treat women like toys,
or the fact that I already know it,
and still I let you in.

I despise you for outsmarting me every time,
and always having the upper hand.
I despise myself for performing and bleeding,
solely for your entertainment.

You are a vindictive predator,
and I am a fool.

My Tears

My tears have washed away the illusion of who I once
was.
The salt of my tears has cleansed the gashes of my
youth.

My tears spoke for me when no one else would,
when I was at a total loss for words.

My tears stroked my cheek when I was afraid,
keeping me company through the nightmares.

My tears held my pain,
carried it far away,
never to return.

My tears showed up when no one else did,
whenever I needed them.
Strength in numbers.

My tears kept my secrets safe in my pillow,
putting them to sleep.

My tears come in all shapes and sizes,
and each one of them is beautiful.

If You Want It

If you want to be loved,
make sure your heart is pure.

If you want to be heard,
make sure you have something worth saying.

If you want more,
you best be giving away all you have.

If you want freedom,
stop confining others.

If you want peace,
stop shouting.

If you want understanding,
step out of your ego.

If you want beauty,
start smiling more.

If you really want that future,
let go of your clutches to the past.

If you want to be appreciated,
humble yourself.
And if all you really want is respect,
then respect your damn self.

Do You Believe Me Now?

I can't rest until I see you again.

My body aches,
My heart is compressed,
I'm choked out.

Your eyes still burn into me,
my heart still beats with yours,
I still use your name.

I miss the music of your voice,
and the way my body never failed to respond to it.

When will these tears stop?
I don't know how I've gone this far without you.

Can you reach me?
Can you hear my heart now?
Please find me.

To see you again is my biggest wish,
you are my only prayer

Speak Up

All your life,
people have been telling you who you are,
what you should become,
and how to get there.
People insist that they know what's best for you,
and that if you just follow their advice,
you'll get there.
Don't listen.

Shed all the outside influence,
and give yourself a chance to speak up.
Be courageous enough to shine through in your own
spritely nature,
regardless of whether you fit the mold or not.
Don't shy away from stumbling and making many
errors,
as long as they are your own.
They will be your signposts to point you in the right
direction.

You were designed to get messy,
live out your questions,
and your life will be your answer.
Think for yourself,
inquire everything,
you may soon realize that you are not at all who you
thought you were,
and that's okay.

Once you've stripped yourself of all the labels,
and old thought patterns,
you give yourself a fresh start.
You are new soil to become who
you were truly made to be,
before everyone else tried to take over.

Grow in your own way.
Who cares if it's crooked,
or odd,
or takes up a lot of space.
Who cares if it outshines people,
or even makes them mad,
because they don't have the guts to follow their own
script.

It's more than okay to be that spunky,
quirky,
insuperable force,
that wildflower that you are.
And when you taste the sweetness of your own fruit,
you'll be so comforted that you
didn't listen to anyone else.

Tummy Rolls

I look at my unruly and crazy hair,
and I smile because it represents my wild side.
I look at my eyes and the pain they hold,
now they are beacons for other hurting people.
They know they can trust me,
because they see I've been there.

I look at my big roughed-up hands,
how they've wiped away the tears of the ones I've loved,
and held the hands of people who've lost everything that
matters to them.
I look at my chubby rolls,
they have kept me warm.
My squishy tummy,
always a soft cushion for my children to lay their sleepy
heads.

My feet have helped me to keep moving forward,
and to walk away,
especially from the people who only liked me because of
what they could take from me.
My freckles and moles,
all constellations,
all over my body.
Not beautiful to everyone,
but I've always liked polka dots.

My scars tell me where I've been,
how each one made me that much stronger.
My skin is sensitive,
just like my heart.
My cheeks are bright,
and intense,
just like my love for you and all of humankind.

My body is the opposite of everything that the
mainstream would call desirable,
but it is my story,
and I love it.
I think if you took the time to read me this way,
you might love me too.

It's A Girl

Two pink lines,
and I thought I was going to pass out on the bathroom
floor.

I didn't tell anyone.
I wasn't ready for this,
how could I ever expect anyone else to be?

I had barely enough to make ends meet as it was,
and I could kiss any chance of a career goodbye for a
long,
long time.
I was still growing up myself,
where did I have the right to teach a child about things
I still haven't mastered?

People nudged me to "take care of it,"
like I was even in the frame of mind to make such a
pivotal decision.
That was the one thing I could never live with.

I struggled mentally for weeks,
my life made no sense anymore.
All my potential doors were sealed shut now.

Then I went to my first appointment.
I was in a total fog of anxiety and panic,
until I saw your heartbeat.

The little light.
Blip.
Blip.
Blip.

There you were,
a little rhythm dancing in me.
And it was that very instant,
I knew exactly why I was put here.
You were not an accident by any means,
you were an earthquake of love.

You were fate stepping in at the perfect moment in time,
pulling me out of a lifetime of misery and emptiness.
You were my answered prayer,
gifted to me before I even got the chance to ask.

I left the hospital knowing I had found everything I'd
ever need,
and I literally had it all,
right inside of me.
You will always be my saving grace.

Déjà Vu

We will meet again,
in another lifetime,
in another existence,
maybe on a Wednesday.

Perhaps by some freak circumstance,
stumbling onto one another.
I'll stare like I always have,
and you'll look at me smiling as if to say,
"what took you so long?"

For hearts like ours are pretty relentless,
and they will not quit,
until they've come home.

About the Author

C. Bager is a chronic daydreamer who lives with her children and dog, she can usually be found with her nose stuck in a book. She loves rocks and snacks, and her life is dedicated to reaching out to those who are suffering and lonely.

Printed in the United States
By Bookmasters